The
PDA Effect

By
Ethan Knight

ᛑ

First published in Great Britain in 2025.
The author has asserted their right under the
Copyright, Designs, and Patent Act 1988 to be
identified as the author of this work.

Paperback ISBN: 978-1-917514-17-0

Edited by Natasha Hawkes
Cover and typesetting by Callum Knight

Copyright © 2025 Frami Books
www.framibooks.com

Dedication

To you, the reader.
Whether you're here to learn, relate,
or support a loved one. Thank you for taking
the time to understand PDA a little better.

I hope this book helps in some way.

Contents

Introduction

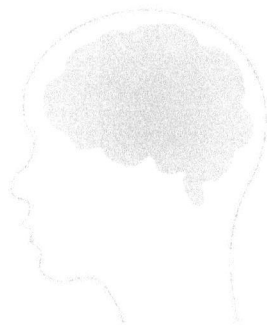

Introduction

Hi, I'm Ethan, and I'm 18 years old. I'm autistic, and I also have Pathological Demand Avoidance (PDA).

PDA is a profile of the autism spectrum, which means it's a way that autism can present itself. It's not a separate condition, but it does have unique challenges—like an intense need for control and a reflexive urge to avoid demands, even the ones I actually want to do. Yes, it's as frustrating as it sounds.

If you've heard of The Secret of My Spectrum by Callum Knight, then you might recognise my last name—because he's my brother, and he encouraged me to write this book. Apparently, one book about autism in the family just wasn't enough!

But in all seriousness, I hope this book will help other families, like mine, understand PDA a little better. Throughout this book, you'll see both autistic and PDA traits in the way I experience the world.

Every autistic person is different, but those of us with PDA struggle with a deep need for autonomy and a really unhelpful instinct to resist anything that feels like an expectation. It can make life interesting, to say the least. I'm writing this book for parents, teachers, friends, and anyone who wants to understand PDA a little better.

My hope is that by sharing my experiences, I can help others feel understood and give families a clearer picture of what living with PDA is really like. So, let's dive in—unless, of course, the idea of reading this now feels like a demand!

Understanding PDA

What It Feels Like for Me

The Struggle of PDA

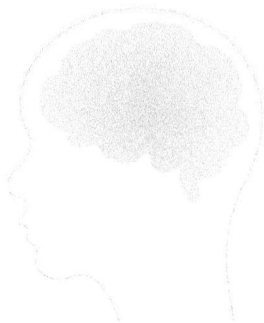

Understanding PDA

What It Feels Like for Me

PDA affects how I see the world. What I want people to understand is that it isn't that I avoid things because I don't want to do them; I don't think about what I do and don't want to do when I refuse to do something. The best way I can think of to describe it is that, to me, avoiding demands is just like breathing.

It's an automatic response that kicks in as a self-protection mechanism; therefore, avoiding decisions feels instinctive rather than being a conscious decision. It's not about being allowed to be difficult or disrespectful; it's about how my brain is wired to respond to different situations.

Even when I want to do something, or I've been looking forward to it, if it suddenly feels

Ethan Knight

like my choice has been taken away, my mind reacts as though it's been taken over by an invisible energy. It really isn't a choice, and I know some people look in from the outside and think I'm being deliberately combative or avoidant and because I've decided to act that way, but I really haven't. Most of the time, I'm just as surprised as they are by my determination to avoid some things.

It's difficult when I've been looking forward to doing something, and then suddenly, my brain shuts down into self-protection mode without warning just because someone has said or done something which has turned it into a demand or expectation.

It could be something simple like brushing my teeth, replying to a text message, or starting a chore, which feels impossible because there seems to be an expectation tied to it, much like being expected to answer a question. My mind starts to process the request, and then suddenly, I feel like I'm holding my breath underwater. When someone is waiting for me to answer them, all I can think about is the pressure I feel pushing down on me.

I can't focus on anything other than how uncomfortable it feels, and then anything they say after that may as well have been spoken in a foreign language because I wouldn't have heard a word of it.

None of this feels like a choice; it feels like my brain has gone rogue and rebelled against my wishes, but it's all subconscious. Sometimes, my mum has asked me if I can't do something because it feels like a demand, but how can I answer that?

All I know is that I can't do it. Is it part of the PDA? I don't honestly know because it feels like it's just a part of who I am; it's completely entwined in how I see myself, the world, and everything else.

The Struggle of PDA

If I could control the PDA, I'd tell it that I'm going to have a lot of fun, or that it's going to make someone really happy or that I might benefit in some way if I do the thing that's been expected or demanded of me, but I can't.

It just doesn't work like that. That's the worst thing about PDA. The more I push myself to go against my instincts, the heavier the request feels, the worse I feel, the worse I react, and the longer it takes me to calm down again.

And all the time, the thought of failing or letting someone down adds to that pressure, which makes me feel bad, frustrated and angry until I want to avoid it completely, so I don't have to put myself through that.

Having control is important to me. If someone tells me to do something, I resist, but when I'm given a choice, like, "Would you rather do this now or later?"—It helps me to feel in control and can prevent anxiety.

Having even a small amount of control makes a huge difference. I often get anxious about not being able to do what's expected of me at the level that I'm expected to do it, and I hate disappointing people, which makes the task even more overwhelming.

What Helps You?

How PDA Affects My Learning

Making Learning Easier
Reducing Pressure and Building Confidence

How PDA Affects My Learning

I have always had learning challenges.
I was ten years old, and I still couldn't read.
My mum tried every single learning system
she could get her hands on, but every single
time, I had a physical outburst, and every part
of my body felt like it wanted to explode. The
frustration was overwhelming.

It feels like I'm trying to open a locked door
without the key, and every attempt I make to
try and engage in the lesson makes my mind
feel more and more confused, like swimming
into deeper water without any armbands on; I
feel alarmed and misunderstood, and that used
to manifest in me as a young child falling on
the floor in floods of tears hitting myself or
the floor.

My brain sometimes struggles to connect
information in a way that makes sense to me.
When I'm working on something that interests

me, my brain soaks up all the information, and I can retain it, but when I'm trying to understand something I have absolutely no interest in, my mind wanders and sometimes literally blanks out on me. It feels like I'm trying to catch a fish with my hands, but it slips away every time.

If I'm feeling controlled, that makes learning much harder.

When I was a kid, my mum enrolled my brother and I into a drama club, and at first, I enjoyed it. I was in the same class as my older brother, and I made a friend. But in the second term, they separated us because my brother's age group had gone into a different class and from then on, I refused to return.

My mum recalls us sitting on chairs outside the room while she tried to convince me to go in, but I had a full-blown screaming meltdown every time, and if she didn't reassure me that I didn't have to go inside, I'd continue screaming until my brother finished his class and came out again. It was a three-hour dance, drama and singing club. I was inconsolable.

It wasn't about the class itself or any of the teachers because they were all kind to me as far as I can remember—I couldn't handle being forced into it, so I shut down. If teachers are strict, it only makes it worse because if I can't make my own decisions, I feel emotionally overwhelmed, and my brain can't cope. Luckily for me, my brother wasn't happy either because he's more socially awkward than I am, and we both asked to leave.

Sometimes, this fear is triggered by not knowing what I'm supposed to be doing. I hate the feeling that other people are getting it, and I'm completely lost, but I also have a deep fear of failure, which has always been a huge part of my resistance to learning.

Making Learning Easier

Learning is much easier for me when I'm given some flexibility. Then, it feels like I'm taking control of my own learning.

If I can work in a way that feels comfortable for me – such as listening to music, using the pen of my choice, or sitting somewhere that doesn't feel awkward or overwhelming – it's easier for me to relax my mind, and that helps me focus on what I'm trying to do.

I realised as I got older that I needed to explain these things to my family. I used to automatically assume they knew what I was thinking and feeling, because in my mind, everyone had the same struggles I did. As a young child, I would get angry and frustrated when I didn't feel considered, especially when I was expected to learn. But once I learned to explain these challenges to my mum, it became easier for us to work together on finding solutions.

I explained that when I'm told how to complete tasks, learning feels like a rigid set of rules with pass-or-fail results, which is too much expectation for me, so I'm compelled to avoid it at all costs.

But when we focus on the learning process instead of just the results, then mistakes don't feel like failures. They feel like hurdles that I can overcome.

When I'm encouraged to concentrate on my learning instead of a competition to get the best result possible, the pressure is off, so I won't get too anxious and want to give up before I start.

So, over the years, I have learned the importance of being happy with small steps forward, which boosts my confidence and makes the impossible feel possible in the future. When I have control over my work, it makes a significant difference.

Reducing Pressure and Building Confidence

Minimise Pressure

When I feel rushed, learning is stressful instead of an opportunity to understand something new. So instead of saying, "You need to finish this now," it helps when I'm encouraged instead. If I'm told, "Take your time; we can finish it later." It makes it easier for me to focus without the added anxiety of working to a time limit.

Breaking Tasks into Smaller Steps Helps

I don't know where to start if all of the information is given to me at once, it becomes something which feels too big and overwhelming. But when things are broken down into small tasks that feel achievable, I can focus on tasks one step at a time which helps me make progress without feeling lost.

Understanding and Compassion

When teachers are patient and don't judge me for struggling with demands, I don't feel too ashamed to ask for help. I need to know that I can try without worrying about getting it wrong, and it helps to be told that making mistakes is the only way to learn.

What Helps You?

Strategies for Support

Ways to Make Things Easier

Praise and Feeling Understood

Ask How You Can Help

Strategies for Support

Ways to Make Things Easier

Make Things More Flexible – Let me choose how I complete tasks, whether that's writing, talking, or using visuals to help me understand and let me work at my own pace.

Focus on Process, Not Perfection – Encourage effort and celebrate small wins to build confidence.

Minimise Pressure – Avoid phrases like "You have to do this now." Instead, try "Take your time" or "I'm here if you want some help."

Allow Autonomy and Control – Give choices, like when to start a task, to help me feel in charge.

Break Tasks into Small Steps – This lessens the chances of being overwhelmed and makes it easier for me to understand and focus.

Be Patient and Understanding – Resistance isn't defiance—it's often a response to feeling controlled.

Offer Emotional Support – Kindness and empathy help me manage frustration and anxiety.

Praise and Feeling Understood

When Praise Feels Uncomfortable

When people praise me, it feels weird and uncomfortable. I know they mean well, but my mind asks why they are judging it at all. It can feel like I'm being scrutinised or watched closely, which makes me avoid it in the future.

I don't want to be praised in front of other people for something which is easy. When I receive praise for something that feels easy or obvious and natural to me, I don't feel proud; instead, I feel awkward and embarrassed. If someone praises me for something that wasn't challenging, I don't appreciate it because it doesn't feel right.

If someone enthusiastically says, "Wow, that's amazing! Well done!" I understand their good intentions, but it feels like over-praising, which makes me feel more pressured the next time I have to complete a task. If I don't meet those expectations the next time, the feeling of failure would be so much worse.

The Kind of Praise That Helps

It's nice when I'm praised for something which has actually challenged me because when I've worked hard on something, I like it when that is noticed, but instead of just saying, "Well done!" at the end, I appreciate it if someone says, "I can see you worked really hard on that." That acknowledgement makes me feel understood. But only if it was a challenge, so it's a good idea to check first.

Don't praise me just for finishing something

easy because it feels strange or uncomfortable. Instead, focus on the challenges I had to overcome or how I solved a problem. That makes me feel like you see the effort I put in. It's not that I don't like praise—I need it to feel true. If people focus on the hard stuff, the things I struggle with, I feel more confident.

The Importance of Feeling Understood

One of the most important things is to feel that someone understands me. It's really hard to do anything if I'm not comfortable with the person asking me, but when I know someone gets me and isn't going to jump to wrongful conclusions about me, then I'm not as afraid to make mistakes, and I'm much more likely to do well.

When I was younger, I used to hide my struggles, and I still do sometimes when I'm around people who wouldn't understand why I find certain things so difficult.

But I didn't have the vocabulary or understanding of myself as a child to be able to explain all this. So, it was really hard knowing that I wasn't like everyone else without knowing why.

When someone tries to understand where I'm coming from, I feel much safer and more willing to try, even if I'm not sure I'll succeed.

When I feel like someone is judging me or doesn't care, I can't focus or feel good about what I'm doing, but if they know that I'm not just being lazy or trying to be difficult, and they can see the effort that I'm putting in, I can relax more and try my best.

How Understanding Makes a Difference

When I am asked privately if there is anything I'm finding challenging or if anything bothering me before I start a task, it makes me feel so much better because it shows that they care about how I am feeling, not just about how I am doing academically. It's important that I don't feel like I'm doing something wrong when I need help, or if I still don't understand, especially when it's already been explained a couple of times.

I don't misunderstand on purpose, and if it takes a few different ways of explaining it before I get it, I need to know that it's okay because I can't control my level of understanding.

As a kid, my mum sometimes explained something a couple of times, and I really didn't get it, so she quickly realised that the task was something I needed to leave and return to days or, in some cases, maybe even years later, because I wasn't at that stage yet.

Some things, like riding my bike and climbing trees, I picked up straight away, but anything to do with letters and numbers took years for me to get to grips with. At first, because I've always been home-educated, my mum told me she felt it was a failure on her part when she wasn't successful in teaching me something new, but as time went on, she started realising that I would learn it eventually. I just needed more time than my brother did, and if she put pressure on me, it only made it harder.

Putting pressure on me, trying to shame me, or making me feel bad about myself for not understanding or learning as fast as you think I should only makes me more demand-avoidant.

It's good to hear. "It's okay if you need time. We'll figure it out together." Here's what I think teachers, or anyone who works with kids, can do to help.

Build a Personal Connection

I need to feel like you care about me as a person first. I need you to acknowledge my challenges. It means a lot when someone can understand how difficult things are for me, even if they haven't experienced it themselves.

Ask How You Can Help

Sometimes, I don't know how to explain what I need, so I need help finding the words to make myself understood.

Options are important; if a teacher or someone says, "What can I do to make this easier for you?" That's an open question and feels overwhelming, but if they ask a question with a yes or no answer, it makes it much easier to communicate effectively rather than just telling me to "get on with it."

Why Asking Questions is So Important

It's so much easier for me to ask for help when I know that I won't be judged if I do.

Asking lots of questions is the best way for me to understand the answer, so if I'm made to feel comfortable enough to ask questions without the other person getting offended or being insulted, then I feel validated and understood. Communication can flow, and mutual understanding can be reached.

If I'm told, "It's okay to ask questions anytime," I feel understood and feeling understood makes me feel a lot more confident, which then makes me less afraid of making mistakes because I know that the people around me are supporting me and want to see me succeed.

Even when I'm still feeling anxious or unsure, if I trust the person I'm working with, asking for help prevents everything from becoming overwhelming, because once that happens, I struggle to communicate effectively and I can't express my needs. It can overwhelm me and sometimes result in a meltdown.

I need to know that it's okay to take a step back and ask for extra support without feeling bad or embarrassed about it, and when people understand that, I'm much more willing to give things a go, even if the task seems too hard in the beginning.

What Helps You?

Friendships and Social Life

My Communication Style Might Be Different

Small, Calm Environments Work Best

Ways to Make Things Easier

Friendships and Social Life

It's always been difficult for me to make and keep friends. It's not that I don't want to have friends, but sometimes, how I interact with people doesn't go the way they expect, which makes me feel like I'm missing something or doing something wrong, even though I haven't intended to.

During a conversation, I struggle to know when it's my turn to speak, and I'm never sure how to join in on a conversation that is already happening between other people.

Sometimes, I feel like I'm watching everything happening as though it's a film, and I'm not involved in what is being said at all. I'm not trying to distance myself; I'm waiting for a pause or a clue to include myself in the conversation, but unless someone asks me a direct question, I find it almost impossible to join in because I'm often stuck, trying to formulate the words in response and by the time I do, the subject of the conversation has already moved on. So I go from looking disinterested in what's being talked about to saying something that has become irrelevant because of the speed of the conversation. I am interested in what other people have to say, but that doesn't always come across. People don't notice the internal struggle I'm having while I'm also trying to figure out how to include myself.

Sometimes, there is so much going on around me, whether that's noise, lights, or more people joining us, that I'm trying to mentally process too much at the same time, which can make things awkward and cause misunderstandings with people.

Especially if there is emotion involved. I don't always know how to show that I care when people are unhappy, even though I do, because I'm too busy processing everything in my mind. My emotions are held back while my brain takes over and is desperately trying to decode what's happening. Not to mention that I'm often too blunt with what I say, which frequently causes people to be offended or angry with what I've said, but my intention is always good, so it leaves me feeling very confused and upset.

This was particularly difficult when I was a child. If people got upset or mad at me, I didn't understand why, and my confusion led to hurt and anger, which led to me feeling sheer rage.

It's also hard for me when people don't understand that I need time by myself. I don't want to offend anyone or seem rude, but socialising sometimes feels too much, so I need some space to recharge.

It's like a phone running out of battery—you need to plug it in and give it some time to get back to full power.

I don't always know how to explain this, so it might look like I'm ignoring people or being uncaring, but I need to take a break to process everything around me.

After a little while of being alone, I can come back feeling more prepared to socialise again. But people don't always see it that way, and that's where misunderstandings come from.

It's also tough when I can't always pick up on social cues, like when someone is joking or when they expect a particular response. I might not realise that someone is being sarcastic, or I might miss the signals that a conversation is ending, which makes things complicated and confusing.

When people are direct with me, I really appreciate it, but when I treat them with the same respect, they think I'm being rude. It's like the same words suddenly have completely different meanings because of the way someone said them, but I only comprehend them one way, so I interpret them in that way.

My Communication Style Might Be Different

I sometimes struggle to find the right words, especially when I feel under pressure, so I might blurt things out and sound rude, even though that's not what I mean. Social expectations can be confusing, so if I go quiet or I'm pretty blunt in our conversations, that's because I don't know how else to respond, not because I don't care.

What Helps Me

- Give me time to process what you say before expecting me to answer.

- Don't take it personally if my tone comes across as blunt—I'm not trying to be rude.

- Understand that in some situations, I communicate better in writing or text rather than face-to-face because I've had more time to process and analyse how I come across.

Clear Communication Helps Me

I really appreciate it when people are clear and direct with me because it makes it much easier to understand what they mean, and I can respond better when I know exactly what someone wants or expects from me.

For example, when someone says, "I'm just joking," or explains the reasoning behind their actions, it helps me understand the situation better, which removes all the guesswork and makes me feel much more comfortable. This is especially important when I'm unsure about the context.

If I know exactly what someone wants from me, I can be myself and join in more easily. It also helps me avoid awkward moments where I might misunderstand what's happening.

Clear and honest communication is crucial to me.

Expect The Best From Me

Never automatically assume I've said something that was meant to hurt or offend someone without checking with me first.

Respecting My Boundaries

When people respect my need for space, it helps me feel less anxious. If I start to feel overwhelmed when I'm socialising, then I need to step away and take a break, but sometimes, it's hard for me to explain why, so it helps if my friends understand I might need time alone after being in a busy or social situation.

That doesn't mean I don't care about the person or don't want to be around them; it just means that I might need to recharge, process and manage how I'm feeling so I can come back when I'm ready. So, I really appreciate it when friends understand that.

Small, Calm Environments Work Best

It becomes overwhelming for me when I'm in a busy or noisy place or when there's too much happening simultaneously.

The noise, the conversations, and the pressure to keep up with what's happening drains me really quickly, and when that happens, my body goes into something like "fight-or-flight" mode.

It feels like a natural response that my body has when something is threatening or overwhelming, but the thing is, my brain sometimes thinks there's a threat, even when there isn't one and when someone demands something of me or puts their expectations on my shoulders, that's when my brain takes over and sends a signal to my body that I am in grave danger.

Sometimes, it feels like everything is closing in on me. My heart races, I feel hot, and my thoughts get all muddled up. Sometimes, the pressure and frustration become so overwhelming that I need to find a way to let it out. The confusion overpowers my rational mind, and I need physical pressure to snap myself out of it, but that feeling is a reaction to the threat of feeling out of control. So, if I feel in control, those threats or demands can't hurt me. I need to know I have a choice and that my autonomy is respected.

This isn't a choice for me. Imagine a car swerves toward you while you're walking across the street—you don't have time to think about it before you react to get out of the way as quickly as possible, and that's what it feels like to me; my body reacts before my brain has time to catch up.

If you can imagine your body having that level of response multiple times a day from ordinary things like talking to people or being in a busy space, you can see how challenging and exhausting being in those situations can be, so I can't help but react in ways that I don't mean to. I might shut down, lash out, withdraw, or even snap at people when I don't want to. But I'm not in control of it. My brain is trying to protect me, even when there's no real danger. That's what makes it so challenging.

I do much better in smaller, quieter environments with less going on than in large groups, and noisy places are challenging for me to cope with.

In a big crowd, it's easy for me to feel lost or like I'm drowning in all the noise, so when I'm in a smaller group or one-on-one with someone, I'm less self-conscious and can connect better without the pressure of being around a lot of people all at once.

Focusing on one person at a time is much easier for me, so I prefer smaller groups or quieter settings when getting to know new

people. I don't like talking about things
that don't interest me; I want meaningful
conversations.

I use woodland walks as a way to unwind.
Being in nature calms my body, mind and
spirit and relaxes me. My dog helps take a
lot of the pressure off; my mum bought him
when I was ten years old because I was having
regular meltdowns, and my anxiety was at an
all-time high because of the situation that was
going on in our life at the time, which we had
no control over. If you've read my brother
Callum's book, 'The Secrets of My Spectrum',
you'll already know that it was his sound
sensitivities and inability to deal with change
when our puppy came to live with us that led
to his autism diagnosis.

So, our dog was an absolute Godsend in
many ways. He's a support dog for me, and
he helped Callum too. I have always loved
dogs, so walking him every day helps me a

lot. When I visit friends and family, and they have a dog, I'm fine; dogs and most animals actually immediately put me at ease.

Predictability and Structure Help Me Cope

I like to know exactly what to expect in advance when spending time with friends. I can't make plans if they're not structured, and predictability leads to a much more enjoyable time. I find it much easier to deal with social situations if I've had time to prepare and if plans are made ahead of time, and I know what's going to happen and who will be there. That gives me a chance to mentally prepare myself, and I feel much less anxious.

On the other hand, spontaneous events or surprises are much harder for me to cope with; it feels like I'm riding a wild horse, and I can't enjoy the experience because I'm too busy clinging on for dear life.

When I was young, I wouldn't even let my family buy and wrap gifts for me because the stress of the surprise was too much for me to cope with. And if there's a social gathering, if I don't know who will be there or what is going to happen, it can be overwhelming and stressful. Whatever the occasion.

I was at a good friend's birthday party when I was six years old, and I remember we were all having a fantastic time until they started setting off fireworks in the back garden. I flew into a panic, and I was in full meltdown mode, crying and covering my ears; my body was shaking, so I had to be taken inside, and I sat with my mum and the family dogs until it was all over.

Patience and Understanding Make a Difference

Sometimes, I find it difficult to understand or connect with people. I know that my reactions aren't always what people expect, and I might pull away when I feel overwhelmed.

But it's helpful when people are patient with me and try to understand where I'm coming from. When friends and family give me space when I need it, communicate clearly, and respect my boundaries, it dramatically affects my feelings. I want to be a good friend and connect with people, but it's just trickier because of how my brain works.

It's not that I don't want to be around people, and it's not that I'm being difficult on purpose—it's just that sometimes, I need things to be a little different to feel comfortable. If you can be patient with me and understand that I need breaks or quiet moments, we'll be able to get along well. I'll be more open, and we'll have a better time together.

It's Not That I Don't Care

At the end of the day, I'm no different to anyone else; I want to be understood, make friends, have a meaningful life, be a part of fun times and share in celebrations with people, but my way of doing it might be a little bit different from others. I'm not trying to be rude, and I'm not trying to push people away. My brain works differently, and the way I process the world can sometimes make things feel overwhelming. So, if you ever find me pulling away or seeming distant, please remember—it's not that I don't care.

I'm just trying to manage everything going on in my head. With a bit of understanding, patience, and respect for my needs, we can build great friendships and enjoy each other's company. And I'll be able to show you how much I care in my own way.

Ways to Make Things Easier

Clear Communication: When people are direct and explain what they need or expect, it helps me understand and respond more efficiently.

Respecting Boundaries: I need space to recharge, especially after social interactions. I need the freedom to say, "I need some time alone," without feeling guilty.

Small, Calm Environments: I do better in quieter settings or smaller groups with less noise and fewer distractions.

Predictable and Structured Plans: Knowing what to expect in advance makes me feel more comfortable and less anxious in social situations.

Patience and Understanding: When people are patient with me and understand that I might react differently or need time alone, it helps me feel less pressured and more connected.

Being Given Time to Process: Sometimes, I need extra time to think through what's happening before I can respond or engage fully.

Honest Feedback: If someone is joking and explains their actions to me, it helps avoid misunderstandings and makes me feel more comfortable.

Quiet Time to Recharge: After socialising or being in a busy place, I need time alone to process and reset. It helps me feel ready for the next interaction.

Non-judgmental Support: When people don't judge me for needing breaks or reacting differently, it helps me to feel accepted and understood.

What Helps You?

Sensitivities

What Overwhelms Me

Touch Can Feel Uncomfortable

Strong Smells Are Too Overpowering

How I Manage All of This

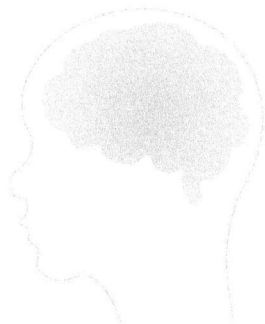

Sensitivities

What Overwhelms Me

As you have learned, living with sensory difficulties isn't easy because my brain and body react to things in ways that might seem unusual to other people. It can feel like the world around me is too loud, too bright, or too intense for my senses to handle.

Everyday things that most people barely notice—like a phone ringing or a flickering light can feel so big and overwhelming that they make me want to shut down or run away.

Even though I want to be part of the world around me, sometimes it's hard to cope with how overwhelming everything feels.

Things that don't considerably affect other people, like fairly loud noises, bright lights, and different textures, can feel unbearable to me.

If I seem irritable, distracted, or like I'm shutting down, it could be because my senses are overloaded.

When I wake up, my senses are turned to the highest setting. Everything feels more intense than it does for most people. Bright lights hurt my eyes, and certain sounds are so loud that they make my body jump.

Sometimes, even the feeling of a tag on my clothes or certain fabrics can feel like they're scratching at my skin, and the distraction overtakes all the other perceptions in my body and mind until I have to remove it.

It's like being in a world where everything is too much, and no one can see that it's too much for me. I don't want to seem strange, but sometimes it's impossible not to react.

For example, when I go to a busy shop or a loud place like a party, it feels like my brain is trying to handle a million things at once.

The PDA Effect

I can hear everyone talking, the music blasting, and even the background hum of the lights above. It's like my brain can't figure out what to focus on, and I start to feel like I might explode.

I don't want to be rude or cause a scene, but all I can think about is how badly I need to leave. The world outside just feels like it's all become too much, and I have to escape.

One of the things that I struggle with the most is noise, and it's not just loud noises like a dog barking or someone shouting, but even little things, like the sound of a phone ringing, people talking all at once, or a car engine, can make my heart race, and my head spin sometimes.

When there are too many sounds going on at the same time, I can't think clearly. It's like my brain tries to listen to everything at once, and it just gets tangled up until I feel overwhelmed, and I need to hide somewhere quiet where I can calm down. As a child, I used to dive under tables when there was nowhere else to hide.

My mum bought a pop-up tent for me when I was young, and I enjoyed spending time in there with my favourite toys.

What Helps Me

- I wear noise-cancelling headphones or earplugs when I need to block out some of the noise. Now, I use music to drown out the sounds that I'm struggling with. If I can't block out the noise, I listen to my favourite songs to help me focus on something more peaceful.

- I avoid places that are noisy or have lots of echoes, like busy cafes or crowded shops and stick to more relaxed environments and quieter places.

Touch Can Feel Uncomfortable

I've already talked about how some fabrics, textures and sensations feel unbearable.
Tags in my clothes, rough fabrics, or even something sticky on my hands will make me highly uncomfortable and I feel overwhelmed. But hugs can also feel too much sometimes. It's not just the proximity of someone else and that they're in my space; there can be so many differing factors that come with it.

Perfume or aftershave can be far too strong for me to deal with and make me feel really sick if someone forces me to inhale it by getting too close, and also the awkward pressure of being hugged in a way that I don't like or for too long.

It's also the expectation, which I dread and I resent it when I'm being judged based on my wish to put myself through that or not.
So, if someone doesn't want a hug or to wear a particular item of clothing, it isn't because

they're trying to cause problems. Even light touches, a tap on the shoulder or a handshake can sometimes feel too intrusive, and I understand that people don't mean to make me feel that way, but I can't control how my body reacts, so if I shrug or back away that doesn't mean I don't like or even love that person, it's a natural reaction for me to preserve my space and autonomy.

My sensory difficulties cause problems, too, because it can mean that on freezing days, I might not want to wear a coat; as a child, this would make my mother crazy, and she used to stress out about it a lot.

She eventually realised that bringing my coat and not trying to persuade me worked better because I was happy to put it on once I was cold.

From the outside, refusing to put a coat on can look like a problem with a lack of discipline, but it's not.

Winter coats and jackets can feel really heavy and restrict my arm movement in a way that makes me feel uncomfortable and panicked. Going into a warm place from outside can make my body suddenly heat up like a furnace, and I feel as though I'm being buried alive in hot sand, so if I don't take it off quickly, I panic and melt down.

What Helps Me

- I pick soft and comfortable clothes and cut off labels.

- I tell people I might not want to be touched, but it does not reflect how I feel about you.

- I use fidget toys or textured objects that feel good in my hands to help me calm down or self-regulate when I feel uncomfortable.

Strong Smells Are Too Overpowering

Strong smells, like perfumes, chemicals, and food, are another issue for me.

Sometimes, I can't think straight because the smell around me is just too much, and it can give me a headache or make me feel sick to my stomach, which affects my appetite and sometimes sends me into demand avoidance too.

I struggle to include myself in these situations, and I'll do anything I can to get out of them because I can't concentrate or focus when everything around me smells strong.
I think my sense of smell must be more sensitive than most people's, or I interpret them more strongly, but I can't ignore it. On the other hand, grass, the earth after rainfall and trees smell amazing to me and help regulate me.

What Helps Me
- I avoid places with powerful smells, like perfume shops, candle stores, or busy restaurants.

- If I'm with people, I ask them to be mindful of wearing strong perfumes or using air fresheners. We don't use chemical air fresheners at home.

Some Foods Are Hard to Eat

Food affects me in different ways. It's not always the taste of the food but the way it feels in my mouth that can be a problem. Some foods have textures that I can't handle, like anything that feels gritty or sticky in my mouth. Even foods I usually like can feel "wrong" on certain days or if they've been put with another ingredient. It's hard to explain, but I can't make myself eat something that doesn't look or feel right.

It's like my brain rejects it before I can even swallow, and when I feel there's no choice other than to eat it, then my PDA kicks in.

For example, beans on toast are in the name, beans on top of the toast. So, as a child if I was served beans next to the toast on my plate or half on top, it wasn't beans on toast. I liked toast cut into small squares and the beans placed on top, covering the toast completely.

As a child, I loved this served in a bowl, and as I grew up, I used plates more. When the food is served in the same way every time, it gives me a sense of peace and safety that helps keep me regulated and feeling in control.

Sometimes, my mum still puts small dishes of food in separate bowls and lets me take what I want. This worked well when she wanted me to try something new because I can't have something on my plate unless I'm going to eat it.

I can't ignore a piece of food on my plate that I have decided I can't eat because then I can't finish it, and the remainder of it makes me feel bad, especially when I know someone has gone out of their way to cook it for me.

How I Manage All of This

Living with all these sensory sensitivities can be really tiring because I'm not just having to deal with the complexity of them, but I'm also then having to find the language skills I need to explain them. People want to know why, and I can't explain all this when I struggle with communication.

Some people automatically assume that I'm just being picky or trying to be difficult, and the dreaded label so many kids get is just being 'naughty'.

Parents are exhausted trying to help regulate their kids, and then they get labelled by others around them as being lazy parents who don't discipline their child or that they're encouraging bad behaviour, but autism and PDA aren't attitude problems or discipline issues. It is a condition which affects our brain and every part of daily life for us. I manage all of this by relying on everyone around me to understand that this condition is a neurological one, not a behavioural one, and everything I do, feel, and experience is sensory and instinctive.

Just as someone else automatically avoids or refuses to take part in something they see as dangerous, I avoid sensory distress and demands. And it's not easy to explain why I struggle or why I react in the way that I do because, along with all this, I have difficulties in communicating.

I don't process language automatically; I need time to think and then format what I want to say to make myself understood properly, making it hard for others to understand. This leads to parents being on high alert almost 24/7. My mum said she realised I wasn't like my older brother when I was around two years old because I didn't engage with her in the same way, I preferred to be in my own little world, and I would run off at every opportunity.

In the end, she bought some reins that she put on me to keep me close and out of danger, which I quite liked because I would lift my feet and swing from it, so not only did she have to hold on, but she also had to keep a tight grip.

Mum said she always had to be prepared for anything, and she couldn't let me out of her sight. I wouldn't listen like my brother did when she told me not to do something, and if the answer to my 'why' wasn't good enough, I took matters into my own hands.

My reactions to things I didn't understand were explosive; I would melt down anywhere at any time.

One very memorable experience was when I was eleven years old. My mum told me not to race my dog to catch the tennis ball; her words were, "If it's a competition between the dog's teeth and your hand, his teeth will win, and you'll get hurt." That was about ten minutes before she was rushing me to the public toilets to rinse off a very bloody hand and assess the damage - which resulted in surgery between my fingers.

Mum recalls how, for many years, she was afraid to sleep at night because she wasn't sure what I'd get up to when I woke up. I woke her up a lot because I always needed help.

So it's really important that more people are aware of the difficulties kids and their families face because you can't teach the autism or PDA out of a child, and you can't shame it out of them, and they definitely can't have it; 'tough loved' or punished out of them, this leads to neurodiverse children with serious trust issues and probably causes severe mental health challenges.

Neurodiversity really needs to be more widely understood in public settings and within public services. It can be isolating and frustrating because I don't want to be judged as rude or difficult. As I've grown up, I've learned a few ways to help myself manage the overwhelm and feel more in control of my world. They don't fix everything, but they can make my life much easier.

Be Mindful of My Sensory Sensitivities: Avoiding strong scents, providing quiet spaces, or not touching me without warning helps a lot.

Let Me Use Sensory Tools: like headphones, sunglasses, or fidget tools, without making a big deal out of it.

Understand That I Might Need to Leave a Situation: It's not because I'm being rude—I need to escape before completely shutting down.

Clear Communication: I've found that it really helps when people are direct with me. If they explain what's going on or what they need, I can understand better and feel more comfortable.

Respecting My Boundaries: I need space to recharge, especially after socialising or being in noisy environments. I need to be able to say, "I need a break," and for people to understand that it's not because I don't care but because I need to manage my energy.

Small, Quiet Environments: I do much better in smaller, quieter spaces. It is easier to focus and I feel less overwhelmed when there are fewer things happening at once.

Predictable Plans: Knowing what to expect helps me feel less anxious. If plans are made in advance, I can mentally prepare for what's coming, which makes it easier to enjoy the experience.

Patience and Understanding: When people are patient with me, it helps a lot because it's not easy for me to explain how I'm feeling all the time, so when people give me the time and space I need, it makes me feel less pressured.

Being Given Time to Process: Sometimes, I need extra time to think about things before I respond or get involved. It helps if people understand that I'm not ignoring them but just taking time to sort through everything.

Honest Feedback: If someone lets me know when they're joking or explains their actions, it helps me avoid confusion and feel more at ease.

Quiet Time to Recharge: After being in a busy or stressful situation, I need time to recharge and process everything. This helps me feel ready to engage again, when I'm ready.

Non-judgmental Support: When people don't judge me for needing space or acting differently, it helps me to feel understood and accepted for who I am.

What Helps You?

Masking, Burnout, and Seeking Support

Masking and Burnout

What Is Autistic Burnout?

When I'm Struggling

Masking, Burnout, and Seeking Support

Masking and Burnout

I don't try to act differently so that I can fit in. I'm not very good at acting because so much of my response is out of my control.

But I do mask my struggles and pretend that everything is fine, even when it's not. When I'm emotional, though, I find it really difficult to mask because I feel like a fizzy bottle that's been shaken up. It's too easy to pop.

I don't force eye contact when it doesn't feel comfortable for me, and I don't copy other people my age because I don't know what I'm supposed to copy.

But, as a child, I was very easily led and trusted what other kids told me. I always wanted to help, so when I was asked by a friend to climb over a neighbour's fence to fetch a ball, I did it, much to my mother's disappointment. I didn't realise that I was supposed to knock on the door first and politely ask for it back; I didn't think about it once I was asked by my friend; I assumed that he wouldn't ask me to do something that was wrong. I can't always tell how I'm supposed to act, and when I try to copy other people, it doesn't feel natural, and I end up feeling lost or confused because I don't know how to act in a way that others expect.

I find it impossible to hide my sensory struggles. The bright lights, loud sounds and the smells that other people might barely notice hit me hard. They overwhelm me, and I can't stop my reactions, no matter how hard I try. And I stim, regardless of who is watching.

Stimming is something I do to help myself feel more in control when everything around me feels too much. It might look like I'm rocking, tapping my fingers, or repeating words to myself. Some people don't understand why I do it, but it helps me calm down when things feel out of control. I can't push through demands. It's just not possible for me. Even though I don't want to upset the people around me. So, pushing me to do something against an instinct of mine leads to overwhelm and, ultimately, a meltdown.

When I try to push myself beyond my limits, it only makes everything worse. And sometimes, even though I don't want to be rude. I can't smile and nod when I don't feel it. It's not that I don't care or that I'm not paying attention; it's that my brain is overloaded, and I can't process it all at once.

What Is Autistic Burnout?

If I pretend I'm okay for a long period of time and push through situations that overwhelm me, even when I don't have the energy, I lose my ability to communicate my needs and end up in something called autistic burnout.

That is when I'm in a state of mental, physical, or emotional exhaustion. When some people have burned themselves out for a long time, it can take weeks or even months to recover.

It happens to me when all the energy I've used to hide my feelings catches up with me. The more I mask what I think and feel, the harder it is to stay in touch with who I am. Over time, the constant need to hold everything in, to appear as though everything is okay drains me and leaves me feeling disconnected, anxious, exhausted and overwhelmed.

I feel lost and tired; it takes everything I've got to keep going. Think about how you feel when you have the flu—too exhausted to move, your brain foggy, and your body aching.

When I'm physically sick, no one expects me to jump out of bed and complete tasks or socialise to push through it, but when my mind is exhausted and needs rest because no one can actually see it for themselves, they often don't realise just how difficult it is to go through, and pushing through when I'm already running on empty, as a child, ended up with me wanting to lash out because I was completely burnt out.

As an adult, I can remove myself from situations that have become too much. But as a child, it was much more difficult if I had to try to explain what was happening and give reasons for meeting my needs to people who often didn't understand.

Often I'm running on nothing, and I'm using all my reserve energy: that's when I become so overwhelmed that it feels impossible to come back from it. I physically can't complete a task, no matter how much I want to. It feels like the world around me is too much, and I can't handle it any more.

I might feel like I need to cry, or hide away in a quiet place to escape from everything. It's not just feeling a little bit tired or stressed.

It's a full-body, panic-level response that I can't control. I feel lost, alone, unsafe and desperately unhappy.

Managing stress, masking, and trying to function in a world that's not built for me means I burn out much faster than other people might. When I shut down suddenly, get irritable or need to withdraw, it's usually because I've reached my limit.

What Helps Me

- Let me rest and recharge without guilt or pressure.

- Understand that my energy levels can fluctuate from day to day.

- Don't assume I can handle it today because I managed something yesterday. Every day is different.

I don't expect people to understand what it's like to live with PDA, but I do hope people will take some time to understand and try to see things from my perspective.

I'm not lazy, rude, or ungrateful—I process the world in a way that makes everything far less accessible to me. When people are patient, flexible, and try to understand, it makes a massive difference in helping me navigate daily life, which will be a huge part of whether I succeed or fail.

When I'm Struggling

When I reach this point of burnout, there are things that can help me feel better.

Taking a Break: When I feel like I'm reaching my limit, it helps if I can take a break. Sometimes, I just need to be alone in a quiet space to reset.

Understanding: It helps when people understand I'm not being difficult on purpose.

Low-Key Activities: After a day of masking, I need calm and quiet activities that don't drain me even more. I like to listen to music, watch a movie, or do something that doesn't require much energy, like walking in the woods with my dog.

Routine and Predictability: Knowing what to expect each day is helpful. When things are unpredictable, it adds to my stress, and I struggle to cope.

Physical Care: When I started putting on weight during lockdown, I focused on lifting weights, which has helped my body and my mental health.

Physical care might include getting enough sleep, eating food that feels good, and making sure I'm staying hydrated. When my body is well taken care of, I have more energy to cope with the mental and emotional stress.

The overwhelming feeling I experience isn't just about being "a bit stressed" or

"frustrated." It's a full-body, panic-level
response that I can't control.

It's not just about "pushing through." I can't
just push through when I'm burnt out. The
best thing someone can do is give me space,
patience, and understanding rather than telling
me to "just deal with it."

It takes time to recover from masking and
burnout, and those around me need to know
I'm not being difficult on purpose.
This isn't fun!

Being kind and patient when I'm struggling
helps more than trying to make me keep going.
I'm doing my best, but sometimes, if my best
just isn't enough, I accept my limits.

What Helps You?

How Parents Can Help

Explaining My Needs to My Family

What I Wish People Understood

Just Because I Seem Fine Doesn't Mean I Am

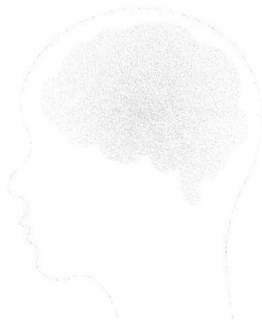

How Parents Can Help

Living with PDA means that my reactions to certain situations can be confusing, especially for my mum and brother. I know that, at times, my behaviour might seem out of place or unreasonable, but I've learned how important it is to explain to them that my reactions are never meant to be rude or disrespectful.

Over time, I've realised that the more I can help my family understand what's going on inside my head, the better we can work together instead of against each other. For example, I might suddenly raise my voice or become sharp when something feels overwhelming.

When that happens, it's not because I'm angry at them but because I feel misunderstood or overwhelmed, and I've had to explain that these reactions are a result of my brain and sensory systems being overloaded, not because I'm trying to be unkind.

I had to explain this, especially to my mum, who sometimes felt I was deliberately hurtful when that wasn't my intention.

Explaining My Needs to My Family

My mum asked me why I always shouted at her when she entered my room, even though she knocked and waited. To her, it seemed like she had done everything right, so when she didn't hear a response, she thought that I couldn't hear her.

But it felt like a sudden invasion of my personal space, and I didn't have time to process it. I had to explain to her that if I'm not prepared for someone to enter my room, I'm caught off guard and struggle to react calmly. It's not about me not respecting her or having anything to hide.

Over time, I've learned how to communicate better with my family about my needs. Here are the things I've learned that really helped when explaining myself to my mum and brother: When I'm in my own space, wherever that is, I need to be in control. Whether that's controlling the lighting, how I structure my time or the layout of my room. It helps me feel less anxious and more in control of my surroundings. Sudden changes, even small ones, can make me feel disoriented and uncomfortable.

Warning me in advance about possible changes, instead of dropping them on me at the last minute, helps me mentally prepare and reduces my stress.

If I'm wearing earphones or ear pods or I'm distracted, switching a light on and off can alert me to someone at my door, which helps me adjust without feeling startled.

This gives me time to prepare mentally and not react impulsively and come across negatively. I've learned to explain that if I react strongly to something that seems small, I'm likely to be overwhelmed. I've shared with my mum and brother that when I get upset, it's often not about what they've said or done; it's about how my brain is processing everything all at once.

I've asked my family to give me more time to think things through. Telling me, "Do you want to talk now or later?" gives me the control to decide when I'm ready, which makes it easier for me to communicate.

My mum would come to us and let us know we were having a family meeting at a particular time so that I could prepare and think of questions and requests.

The best conversations often happen while walking the dog because I'm naturally calmer and more relaxed.

Sudden Demands Don't Work for Me

Even small requests can feel overwhelming

and demanding if they come too suddenly. Something as simple as "Can you come downstairs?" can make me feel under pressure. Instead, when given options or explanations, I feel more in control. For example, if someone says, "Will you come downstairs because..." This makes it easier for me because I know what to expect.

My Reactions Aren't About You

My sharp tone or sudden reactions don't reflect how I feel about the other person; they're not personal. It's just how my brain and body respond to being overwhelmed. So, staying calm and giving me space to reset helps me to regain control.

What I Wish People Understood

I Need to Feel in Control

Living with PDA means that I experience the world differently from others.

I know that my reactions often don't make sense to other people. Sometimes, I might seem resistant, uncooperative, or even rude when that's not my intention at all. I'm not trying to make life harder; I have a brain that responds to demands and expectations in ways that are beyond my control.

And I wish people could see I'm genuinely trying my best beneath those reactions.

Here are some things that would help me feel understood, supported, and more comfortable in everyday situations: Like a lot of autistic people, the world often feels unpredictable and overwhelming to me, but add PDA to that, and when I don't have control over my environment or the plans that are made on my behalf, my brain switches to panic mode, and that's why I sometimes react so strongly to what might seem like a small thing to other people like someone entering my room unexpectedly or sudden change in plans.

What Helps Me

- Let me know about any changes ahead of time.

- Give me control over little things, like where I sit or how I approach a task.

- Ask for my input before making decisions on my behalf.

Just Because I Seem Fine Doesn't Mean I Am

I'm good at masking my feelings when I'm struggling so that I don't stand out or feel vulnerable, which is why it's so important to feel safe around the people in my space.

I don't like people coming into my home if I don't know them because trust isn't something I give freely.

But masking is exhausting, and just because I look like I'm managing it doesn't mean I'm okay. I might appear calm, even happy, while inside, my brain is in full panic mode.

What Helps Me

- Check with me privately rather than assume I'm okay because I'm quiet or not responding.

- Understand that I might need time to recover after social situations or challenging tasks.

- Let me take breaks when needed so I can reset.

I'm Not Doing It on Purpose

When I seem resistant, whether to a request, a task, or even answering a question, it's not because I don't care or because I'm trying to be difficult.

PDA triggers an overwhelming sense of panic and pressure when I'm told what to do, even when I want to do it. It's not something I can turn off—it's a reflex.

Offer me options instead of making demands,

like, "Would you like to do this now or in five minutes?" Frame things as a suggestion or a collaboration instead of an order.

Give me time to process instead of rushing me for an immediate response.

What Helps You?

Final Thoughts

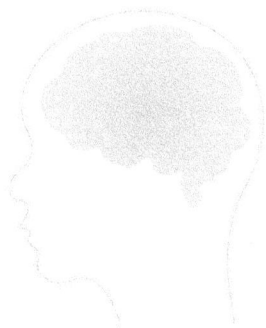

Final Thoughts

Living with PDA, autism, and learning difficulties is challenging, but I'm learning to cope better every day. Getting older hasn't automatically made things easier; some things are much harder because I sometimes feel like I'm being left behind when so many other kids my age are beginning their adult lives.

My anxiety is so bad that some days, I can't leave the house by myself because I've convinced myself that something terrible will happen.

I know everyone experiences the world differently, but just because my experiences are different doesn't mean they're any less valid than anyone else's. By being kind to myself and asking for the help I need, I can navigate life in a way that feels safer and more manageable.

I need a lot of help right now, but I've seen

huge improvements in my ability, going from a child who couldn't read at ten to studying GCSEs online and writing this book.

If you're young and struggling to learn, don't feel bad. Things do start to make sense eventually. But if you push yourself before you're ready, you only set yourself up to fail. I know what it feels like to judge yourself harshly, think you're stupid or lazy, and feel confused about yourself and why you act or feel a certain way.

Whether you have an official diagnosis or not, it isn't easy to feel like you belong in a world that doesn't always understand your difficulties. But that doesn't mean you're not intelligent. It doesn't mean you won't learn it.

You might need more time than others, but learning is a process—and it's happening from the moment we're born until the day we die. So, take each day as it comes, and be kind to yourself.

Along the way, I've learned the importance of helping my family understand how my brain works and how I process the world. Once they understood me, life became much easier.

Too many people around me had assumed that I was being deliberately combative or avoidant while growing up, so having a family who supported me made a huge difference. When other people understand my needs, I feel safer and more supported, and I'm able to navigate the world with less stress and anxiety.

Don't give up if, like me, you struggle to express your feelings in words. Look through what I've written, highlight the parts you can relate to, and then show them to the people you trust. Help them understand that PDA isn't something that can be trained out of us. It's a part of us, and we need help to live with it.

Organisations and Support Groups

United Kingdom

PDA Society
Provides information, support, and training for individuals, families, and professionals dealing with Pathological Demand Avoidance. snapcharity.org

National Autistic Society
Offers guidance on demand avoidance and supports autistic individuals and their families. autism.org.uk

PDA Support Lancs
A support group for families with children and young people with a PDA profile of autism within Lancashire, offering regular meet-ups both online and around the region. pdasupportlancs.org

PAST (PDA Support Team)
Provides one-to-one consultations, support
groups, and training for parents, carers, and
professionals to effectively support individuals
with PDAs.
p-ast.co.uk

Contact
Offers information, support, and advice for
families with disabled children, including
those affected by PDA.
contact.org.uk

United States

PDA North America
Dedicated to spreading awareness and
understanding of PDA, offering resources,
support groups, and training for parents,
individuals, educators, and therapists
throughout North America.
pdanorthamerica.org

Journeys With PDA
Provides advocacy, training, and support for

those living and working with individuals
with a PDA profile, including free support and
connection chat groups.
journeyswithpda.com

At Peace Parents

Offers coaching and support for parents of
PDA children and teens, helping families gain
clarity and bring more peace to their lives.
atpeaceparents.com

Parents Helping Parents (PHP) – Autism
with PDA Support Group

A support group where parents can talk with
others who share similar family dynamics,
appropriate for those with school-aged
children and young adults.
php.com

PDA Parents

A resource hub offering information and
support for parents navigating PDA, including
connections to other organisations and
advocates.
pdaparents.com

Ethan Knight — Author

Struggling with learning and speech difficulties throughout his childhood, Ethan couldn't read until the age of ten. His journey to becoming an author has been shaped by perseverance, resilience, and a deep desire to share his lived experiences.

Having overcome challenges that once made everyday communication difficult, he now aims to help others better understand the unique struggles and strengths of people like him. He has a passion for medieval British history and weightlifting—because if he has to carry the burden of constant demand avoidance, he may as well build some muscle while he's at it.

Books we think you'll like

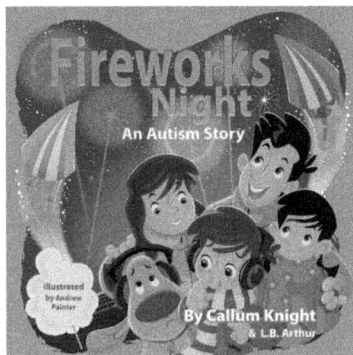

Framibooks.com

www.ingramcontent.com/pod-product-compliance
Lightning Source LLC
Chambersburg PA
CBHW051247020426
42333CB00025B/3100